prayers

Sylvia Browne

Hay House, Inc.
Carlsbad, California • Sydney, Australia
Canada • Hong Kong • United Kingdom

Published and distributed in the United States by:
Hay House, Inc., P.O. Box 5100, Carlsbad, CA 92018-5100
(800) 654-5126 • (800) 650-5115 (fax)
Hay House Australia Pty Ltd., P.O. Box 515, Brighton–Le–Sands
NSW 2216 1800 023 516 • *e-mai:* info@hayhouse.com.au

Editorial: Jill Kramer • *Cover Design:* Christy Salinas and Ashley Parsons
Interior Design: Ashley Parsons • *Illustrations:* Christina Simonds and
Leonid Gore

Library of Congress Cataloging-in-Publication Data

Browne, Sylvia.
     Prayers / Sylvia Browne.
          p. cm.
     ISBN 1-56170-902-6 (hardcover)
     1. Prayers. 2. Society of Novus Spiritus (Campbell, Calif.)—Prayers-
books and devotions—English. I. Title.

BF1311.P67 B76 2002
299'.93—dc21

                                        2002039691

ISBN 1-56170-902-6

05 04 03 02   5 4 3 2
1st printing, February 2002
2nd printing, March 2002

Printed in China by Palace Press

This book is

dedicated

to all the ministers

and study groups

around the country.

— Sylvia Browne

I dedicate the angel drawings in this book
to our precious Sylvia, who has helped to
make my dreams come true, opened the
hearts and minds of us all, and filled my
soul with everlasting love for our Beloved
Mother and Father God . . . and to my angels,
who have guided me down this path
and stood still long enough
for me to draw them.

— **Christina Simonds**

contents

preface

Over many years of public work, people have often asked me how to pray. My answer is simple: "Just talk to God, and make your life a living prayer." In fact, your actions in life carry far more importance than merely speaking some words. We all know people who *say* the right things but who *do* the wrong things. The best way to pray is with your actions; doing what's right is the best prayer. Being kind, caring for others, and helping those in need are the prayers that God really wants to hear. We will eventually judge ourselves by what we *did* in life, not by what we said.

The following pages are taken from my sermons, delivered at my church, Society of Novus Spiritus. In each case, the words were "infused" into me by my spirit guide Francine, and of course, by God. Granted, these words are a passive mode of prayer, yet the goal is to recharge your spiritual battery so that you'll be able to go out into the world and do God's work. As you will see as you read, there is no condemnation, judgment, or demeaning of your soul. You are *not* a sinner; all people are worthy in the eyes of God. As such, many of these prayers begin with "Beloved Creator . . ." as is befitting a loving relationship with God that is continuous and eternal.

I assure you that these words, as simplistic as they sound, will elevate and expand your soul. You will realize your self-worth so that God's love can pour directly into your thirsty soul. Our society tends to infect us with "you're not worthy" germs, which sets up a negative block to accepting God's light. These prayers will help you remove that negative block.

God is perfect, all-loving, and constant. Therefore, God cannot have any of the human traits of being mean, petty, or hateful.

On your spiritual journey through life, you should certainly take the time to speak with God—in your own words, in your own way. I encourage you to borrow the words in this book as a starting point, but I expect that you will change them into a more comfortable form better suited to your own style. I hope that these prayers will give you more confidence in yourself, and in your right to speak directly to God.

Try to be open to the idea of a "Mother God." We call Her "Azna," but any loving name is appropriate. Also, the Holy Spirit is a very real force in the world; it is the power of Divine love, and we call upon it often for help. We have lots of protection to call upon while we're here: Father God, Mother God, the Holy Spirit, Jesus, angels, spirit guides, and many more. Include all of these beings in your prayers. They will help you.

These prayers will lift your soul and let you magnify the Lord. They have done so for me and thousands of others. Many miracles have occurred through the power of prayer, and now I want to share these commanding words with you.

Enjoy the life that God has given you, and realize that you have chosen to manifest God's love in this world. Make every action, every day, your prayer to God.

God love you . . . I do.
— Sylvia

the
prayers

prayer for

jubilation
and
thanksgiving

(Should be said every morning on a daily basis)

Praise be to the Creators.
Praise be to Mother and Father God.
Praise be to Their Holy and Sacred Names.
Praise be to the Life-Givers.
Praise be to the positive and joyful givers.
We ask that our souls be filled with
Your love today, with Your omnipotent grace.
Praise be Your Holy Names.
Fill my heart with love, and where there is love,
there can be no taint of despair,
greed, or negativity.
Praise be Your Holy Names.

morning prayer

Dearest Mother, protect and guide me throughout this day. Oversee all my actions so they will be in accordance with my chart, which has been a Divine contract between our Father in heaven and myself. Keep my thoughts filled with the holiness of Thy will, and knowing this, I will have joy in my heart. Amen.

prayer for
midday

Dearest Mother, the ruler of the earth and the day, allow the love that flows from You to the Father surround me. Restore my energy and allow me enjoy each moment. I pause now and breathe deeply, closing my eyes and allowing Your Divine love to purify and rejuvenate me. Amen.

evening or before bed

Dearest Mother and Father, the day is finished—a day like so many that I have lived, and many more that I may live within Your blessed grace and light. As Your mantle of darkness falls, let peace come into my heart and all despair be replaced by joy. I know that I have completed another day in Your service. I call on all the blessed angels and the Christ-consciousness to attend to me and bring me peaceful sleep and blessed dreams. Amen.

ourselves and the world

Dearest Mother and Father God, surround us today with the Christ-consciousness and the feeling of the Holy Spirit that is descending upon us. We ask for grace during this spe- cial time in which peace will descend upon our hearts, and God's power will be stronger in us than it has ever been. We ask a miracle for ourselves and those we love—anyone we are worried about. Let us send out the sparks from our hearts and souls to encompass all our loved ones.

All the people who have gone before, we ask them to attend to us, give us grace and hope, and walk with their hand in ours. Let us lift up our worries and give it to God; be it loneliness, depression, worry over a son or daughter, or a health problem. If someone is in pain, we ask that God be merciful and let them leave. We ask that there will be peace in the world, that there will be a conscious effort not to destroy and pillage, and that there will be no more prejudice. We ask that the fighting stop, the homeless find homes, and that the love of God visits every man, woman, and child today.

We ask that we as a group can be as powerful as we wish to be and as strong as we know we can be, sending out our light to the world—not necessarily to convert, but to help, to be the silent comforter—so that someone standing on a lonely street corner gets a shot of our love. They don't have to know where it came from; they will simply get a spark of hope and a renewal in their faith.

We ask that our lives from this point on be easier, that our strength increases, and that our finances and health improve. We ask this not only for ourselves, but for the whole world. We ask that we all be protected from harm, and we ask for a healing for everyone.

We ask this in the name of the Mother, Father, Son, and the Holy Spirit. Amen.

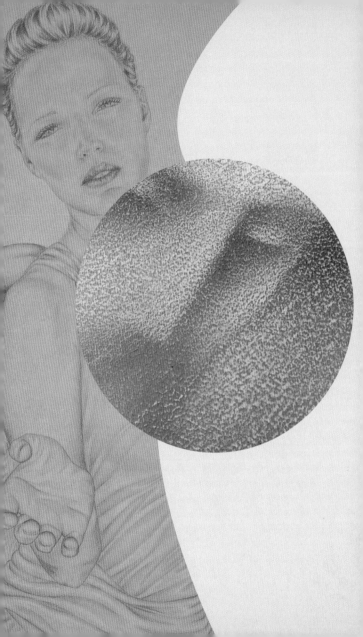

release of pain

Dear Mother and Father God, hold me in Your hands. Stroke away all the pain that resides in my body. Increase my intellect to override the ravages of this life. Send Your angels to comfort me. I ask that the archetypes encase my pain and alleviate all suffering. I also ask for and expect not only a healing, but a miracle. Dear Mother, Queen of the Universe, attend to me now and give me peace of mind, body and soul. I expect the peace to come now. I *am* of sound body, mind, and soul. Amen.

healing prayer
of Novus Spiritus

(May be said alone or in a group)

Dear Mother and Father God, we are all gathered here to love You and to receive Your blessing and healing energies. We ask that You send Your everlasting energy to heal all who are in need today, using the healing force that You, as our omnipotent Parents can provide. Send us all the power and force of Your energy and love to heal us all, to sustain us in our everyday lives so that we can continue to experience for You. Help us to remain examples of Your love, and guide us back to You if ever we go astray from our chosen paths. Loving Mother and Father, help all of our Spirit

Guides to channel Your energy and the energy of the archetypes that surround this gathering in Your name so that the energy sent is received fully and completely in each and every one of us. For those loved ones who are unable to gather with us today, we also ask that You send them Your healing energy and love so that any malady, whether it be mental or physical, be completely healed and eliminated.

We ask for this in Your name, Mother and Father—the name of God. Amen.

Arem, Shem, Beth, Sedal, Sacravalian, Ahad.

(Translation: *Blessed be this Queen on high that is sacred to all who come to Her.*)

Novus Spiritus communion prayer

Dear Mother and Father God, I ask You to witness this communion, which is a symbol of finding my very own God-centeredness and Christ-consciousness. I am impressing on my higher consciousness that I am dedicating my life to God's will. The symbol of this communion for me through Novus Spiritus means that I wish to be born into the New Spirit of true spirituality and let go of all the guilt and karma of our past lives and start fresh and new. From this time forward, I will be on track, fulfilling my theme and walking with the blessed aura of God's light. I do this as an activation of my will to symbolize to myself and the world that I walk with grace, free of all negativity.

We ask this in Your name. Amen.

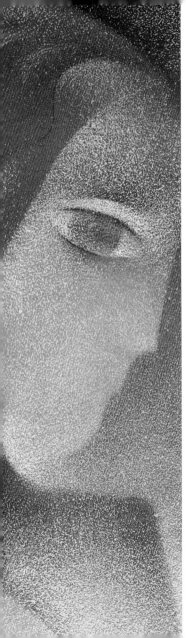

relationships

Dear Mother and Father, I send my petition directly to Your heart. I ask that I find a kindred soul as a partner for my life. I ask that a perfect partner who shares my beliefs and devotion to You surface in my life. I will allow no negativity to block this. I will be patient because I know everything happens in Your Divine plan. Please send me a perfect mate in mind, body, and soul. Amen.

25

blessing
of the
children

Dear Mother and
Father God,
we ask today
that blessings be
bestowed upon
these children that
stand before You.
Let Your light of healing,
morality, and righteous-
ness shine upon their souls
today. Let not the roots
or tentacles of darkness
come near their souls.
Let not any temptation
or addiction be part of
their life's plan. Keep their
souls under constant
watch and protection
so that no darkness

comes into their sphere of consciousness. Bless and guide them to stay on track and bring about all that is good in their lives and those of others. Bless their lives so they will be endowed with purpose and courage, and instill within their souls on this day the light of everlasting grace. Amen.

prayer for

protection of the children

Dearest Mother, since You are the creator of all with our Holy Father, please protect our children. Protect us, also, as we are Your children. Keep our children from any bodily or physical harm. Keep Your mantle of protection around them. Infuse them with the knowledge of what is right and wrong. Keep them from all illegal activities or addictions with the help of Your holy grace. Protect and help them walk in Your holy spiritual light. Amen.

prayer for

spiritual baptism

Let it be known that God is not only with us, He is *in* us! His life is infused into all. Embrace His love as you trust that His power is real in your daily life. Let us pray.

Lord, keep us in the stream of Your Holy Spirit so that the flow will saturate our lives. We thank You for working in us so that we can live in You. The Spirit Himself bears witness with our spirit that we are children of God. God's Spirit leads and convicts us. The fruit of this Spirit is love, joy, peace, patience, kindness, goodness, faithfulness, gentleness, and self-control. Amen.

prayer for

fortitude as parents

Dearest Mother and Father, help me understand, love, and even forgive my parents. Help me to understand all the roads I've chosen and what lessons I've learned. Also, help me to be a good parent. Give me the ability to be fair and loving, and a giver of spiritual love and guidance. You are my ultimate parents. Help me to be as close to Your example as humanly possible. Give me patience and understanding. I ask for this to be revealed to me by Your holy will. Amen.

prayer for

aging

Dear Mother and Father God, as I grow older, let me be more patient and tolerant. Allow me by Your heavenly grace to view my life through positive eyes. Let me see my life as a spiritual journey for my perfection and experiencing for You. Let me view life as a song that has a beautiful melody and not be tainted by grief, guilt, and the false hopes of what I should have been. Let me grow in wisdom, endurance, and courage so I can stand before You and feel proud that I have been a light to many in a lonely desert. Amen.

benediction—
a Gnostic blessing

Blessed be God, the Father,
Blessed be His holy name.

Blessed be the name of Azna,
Blessed be Her holy name.

Blessed be the name of our Lord, Jesus Christ,
Blessed be his holy name.

Blessed be the archetypes that protect us,
Blessed be their holy names.

Blessed be our spirit guides,
Blessed be all their holy names.

Blessed be everyone here today,
Blessed be all our names.

Blessed be our loved ones not present,
Blessed be all their names.

Amen.

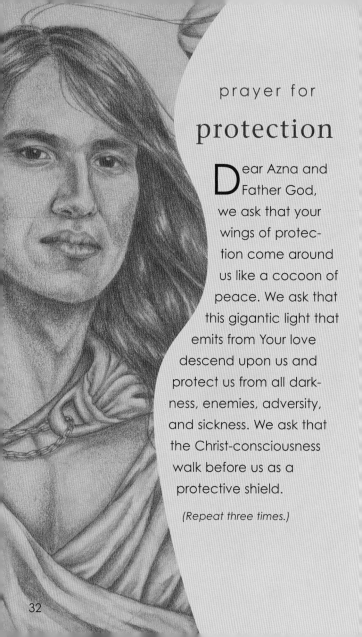

prayer for

protection

Dear Azna and Father God, we ask that your wings of protection come around us like a cocoon of peace. We ask that this gigantic light that emits from Your love descend upon us and protect us from all darkness, enemies, adversity, and sickness. We ask that the Christ-consciousness walk before us as a protective shield.

(Repeat three times.)

remain steadfast throughout this life

Dearest Mother and Father God, we ask for all the people who have loved us, whom we love, to be cared for. We ask for the Christ-consciousness to come into our hearts. We ask that our souls be insulated through this year—to be full of grace and to be convicted to our beliefs and be able to share them. Even more important than sharing our beliefs is to *live* them, which is more difficult than it may seem. We ask that we have health and that we can face adversity and grief with strength, fervor, and knowledge. As morbid as it sounds, but as jubilant as it is, this life will eventually end, and we will be thankful that we will all be reunited in God's time, in the true Holy Land, which is the Other Side. We ask for an acceleration of our work for God, of researching and finding our true way back Home.

We ask this in the name of the Mother, Father, Holy Spirit, and the Christ-consciousness. We ask for all the archangels and archetypes to surround us and to stay steadfast with us, and for our spirit guides to be sentient figures. We ask this in all Their holy names. Amen.

prayer to

be a shining example

My Beloved Mother and Father God,
please imbue me with:

Loyalty—
to be loyal and true to my own
beliefs, true to myself.

Gratitude—
to be grateful that I am here and
able to learn, knowing that only
the strongest are allowed to come here.
Let me be thankful for my perfection.

Honor—
imbue me with honor, right actions,
protocol, and right speech. I will treat
others with honor for the spark of
God they carry. I will honor my
temple as well, by taking care of myself.

Truth—

to know my beliefs and to
live them. To thine own self be true.

Love—

to attain love of self and love of coming into life.
Love to do battle for God and to know that spiri-
tuality is simply doing a kindness every day.
To love the unique spark of God within.

Pride—

to know pride in oneself is good.
I take pride in myself and
protect my spark of God.

For this I pray so that I may
be a shining example of Your love
and light in this world. I ask this all
in the name of God.
Amen.

spirituality
prayer

Dear Mother and Father God, I ask for the mantle of Mother God to descend upon me and open my heart to the truth and the knowledge of Gnosis. I ask for the Divine and intellectual knowledge of God the Father to not only stimulate my intellect, but to weld my emotions together so that I become like a point of light that illuminates many. But in so doing, I become illuminated by the wealth and infusion of knowledge that You will give unto me for the asking.

I will walk each day in the light of the Holy Spirit. I will be a defender against darkness. I will not allow any grayness to enter my soul. I will have the right words to speak to those who ask for my knowledge and my truth. I will be a lighthouse that beckons to many. I will have an eternal light of love, perception, and knowledge.

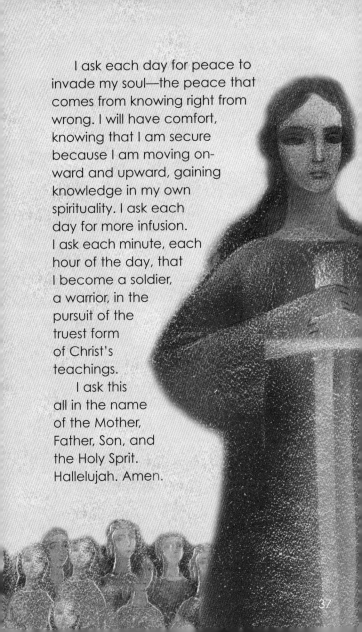

I ask each day for peace to invade my soul—the peace that comes from knowing right from wrong. I will have comfort, knowing that I am secure because I am moving on-ward and upward, gaining knowledge in my own spirituality. I ask each day for more infusion. I ask each minute, each hour of the day, that I become a soldier, a warrior, in the pursuit of the truest form of Christ's teachings.

I ask this all in the name of the Mother, Father, Son, and the Holy Sprit. Hallelujah. Amen.

prayer for

strength of our truth

Dear God, we ask for Your immediacy in giving a blessing to us today. We ask for the Mother God to wrap us in Her mantle of protection. We ask for the Christ-consciousness, clear and beautiful, tall and strong, to walk beside us and in our hearts. Let no man or woman spoil the fact that we are now pure of heart and pure of spirit, and that we will let go of all the prejudicial things: the bigotry, the hurt, the guilt, and the fear. In removing that, we ask to stand before God as a shining, pure example and a crystal light, and we ask only for strength and fortitude.

We ask for a funnel by which our spirituality comes through. We ask to feel the warm baptism of healing coming directly from the Mother God Who is the Great Interceptor; from Christ,

Who was the Anointed One on this earth; and from the Father God, Who holds us continuously in His hand. We ask that the journey be made easier, and most of all, that we have the strength of conviction and are witnesses to the truth.

Let us say in our heart, "Blessed be Thy name," and not be afraid to say, "God, I love You. You are my ultimate Lover, Creator, Consummator, Healer, Benefactor; and all of this is for You."

And when it comes time for us to go, we ask to be able to cross over that threshold blissfully, happily, and in the presence of Your marvelous and magnificent force, and to carry the Christ-consciousness, the embodiment of Christ, with us in this life.

I ask this in the name of the Mother, the Father, the Son, and the Holy Spirit's Light that guides me through this dark world. Amen.

salve for the
soul prayer

My Beloved Creator, may I feel the power of the White Light around me and dredge up from my soul, from my consciousness, the lower mind, all unforgiveness, and simply allow others to be. Things that have been done to me, the things that maybe I have done, let me allow myself to accept all of this and go on. May I feel the peace coming from Mother God, wrapping Her mantle around me. Let me feel the peace coming from Father God, in wisdom and static continuous love, holding me forever in His hands. And may I feel the blessings of all the prophets, all the saints who went on before me, the archangels that attend me, and my guides that stand as silent, stalwart figures. I ask the Council that sits on the Other Side to help me through my life's plan.

I pray for a balm, a salve that Mother God can rub over my soul to heal the pain, heal the hurt. I know that I can say to myself, "It's all right for me to prevent that person or situation from coming into my life again." Take my hands and smooth out my aura that has been punctured and hurt by a friend, loved one, or relative, which can be the cruelest blow. May I let it go and allow it to be, unconditionally feeling how unfettered I am, how unchained. May I feel Mother God, Father God, and my guides standing with me, and know I am never alone. Amen.

prayer for
infusion

Dearest Mother and Father God, send the Christ-consciousness to me to infuse Your Holy Will. Let all my words be measured with love and judgment. Allow knowledge to come through me. Let my words be Your words of wisdom and comfort. Let me be enlightened in all my senses so I can help myself as well as others. I will meditate on the aspect that I am a golden tube of truth and awareness, and that I will not fail in service to You, myself, and others. Amen.

prayer to
make yourself aware of a higher power

Dear Mother and Father God, I know I am never alone. You are always with me. My soul, my identity—that something that says, "I am I" to me—is an eternal gift from God, the Great

Intelligence. I can never lose myself, because this self is a part of God. I am a part of God; and God—Mother and Father—have a great purpose in life for me, which They will reveal day by day as I grow in strength of body, mind, and spirit. I am well and strong. I have the power to overcome all things within me. In God's care, no harm can befall me. I now give myself over to Mother and Father God's protection and will follow Their guidance day by day. Amen.

safe travel

Dear Mother and Father God, please keep me safe. Keep the archangels' power of light around me. Place pillars of light around any and all transportation. Mother, keep Your mantle around me so that there will be no mishaps or accidents for me and my loved ones. Regardless of whether it be by plane, train, car, or by any means, keep us all safe in Your arms. Amen.

prayer for

purification and renewal

Dearest God, surround me with the White Light of the Holy Spirit. Let me feel Your quiet peace, Mother and Father, invading my heart, mind, and soul—and the Christ-consciousness pulled into my very being. May I feel the light emanating from me into the heart of every other person. My life, like a highway in which I am traveling, can seem cluttered with all kinds of flotsam and jetsam of all my past lives, and even with what I am going through in this life. But with my strength, my symbol, a light, a sword, or my totem, let me sweep that pathway clean. Feeling that everything in my life is clear-cut and straightforward, nothing can impede my growth. I ask for my needs to be met, but more important and above all, for my spiritual growth and for my soul to magnify the Lord. I ask for it to stretch my wings inside and embrace my truth, my vision, and my belief. May I look back down the highway and may it now be clean. Ahead of me may be clutter, but strengthen me, Dear Lord, against illness, against adversity, against any programming that may come from outside of myself—so that I may walk with courage.

May I feel myself being healed from all wounds that are slung at me. Like the slings and arrows of outrageous fortune that hit, I am impervious to all, because I walk with my hand in God's—truly unfettered, clear in mind and body, pure and loving in motive, and devout in soul.

I ask this in the name of the Mother, the Father, the Son, and the Holy Spirit. Amen.

prayer for

self-esteem

Dear Mother and Father God, let my true essence shine through. Let the true beauty of my soul bloom in Thy sight. Let the Christ-consciousness show me not only my purpose, but also the estimation of my true self. Let me not be fettered by false ego, but rather allow me to bask in my own spiritual essence, which is my truth and my purpose.

Do not allow me to fail by false guilt and false criticism. Let my essence magnify Your will, and help me live my life of spiritual service. Amen.

spring equinox prayer:

morning

Dearest Mother Azna, in this time of Spring Equinox, we bring to you all things living and growing. These offerings (plants and seedlings) are a symbol of the growth within our own souls.

To show our love and devotion, we offer these tokens, oh dearest Azna. Help us grow in wisdom and grace in the fertile garden of your beneficence.

Each seedling represents our souls reaching through the negativity of this planet and stretching toward our fulfillment and Gnostic enlightenment.

Help us through this month, this year, and all the days of our life to honor and adore you. Intercede for us to the Father, and make our journey of life easier. Amen.

spring equinox prayer:

evening

Dearest Azna, accept our petitions. We are soliciting your help in aiding us in our quest for protection. We know that our petitions will be granted, whether they are for our mental, spiritual, or physical self. We know that with Your help, we will be more sanctified with these petitions.

We ask for Your Divine intercession, to help us in all ways, thereby ensuring that we also keep our love and devotion to You steadfast and unwavering.

Blessed be the name of the Father, Mother, the Christ-consciousness, and the Holy Spirit. Sanctify us and this day of joy. Amen.

prayer for

animals

Dearest Christ-consciousness and Mother and Father God, please protect all living things. Protect all the animals of this planet. Allow them to live with love and peace. Keep them safe from persecution and experimentation. Keep them from being cold and abandoned. Help the world to understand that this is all part of Your creation. Make humanity understand that we must *all* live in harmony. Amen.

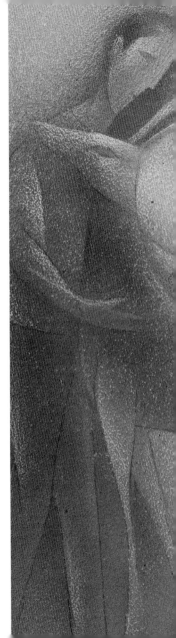

bringing up the true
estimation of self

My beloved Creator, totally encompass me in Your beautiful golden light. Help me to clear my mind of all darkness and all cobwebs. Let me feel and see our Lord approaching—beautiful as light, glowing, huge dark eyes, coppery skin, flowing hair, clean-shaven, tall, slender, sweetness from light and love emanating. Arms outstretched, walking toward me, giving me the blessing, the truth, and the light. The consciousness, the bearing witness to, reaching up for his lips, which come down to kiss me. I ask to drink of the knowledge from the lips of the Lord. Behind the glowing silhouette are Father and Mother God—bright, shining, omnipotent, loving, and glowing with circles of light.

Let our Lord reach his hands out to me, grasp me, and hold my hand. Let me feel this current of protection, and let all pain and suffering disappear. Miracles are accomplished through this. Let me know that I, and I alone, am so important that I am a link in the Divine chain; that I am part of the genetics of God, created from God's genetics. As a spark of the Divine, I am symbiotic with Christ, with all the prophets, with all the greatness.

Let me feel strength, peace, gratitude, loyalty, and harmony—I ask this in the name of Mother and Father God. Amen.

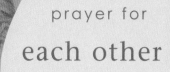

prayer for

each other

Dear God,
I pray that
we be strong
and wise and
courageous.
Let us be
ready, O God,
to fight the
terrible darkness
of a lonely night.
Our shield is our
faith and knowledge
in You. We shall face
many adversities in
the arena of life;
those watching
us may shout
"heretic"
or "saint,"

but the truth is known only to us and You.

We stand before You, dearest, sweet God; please do not remove Thy hand. We do not care for glory or fame. We are only the plumage that carries Your name. We do not fear false ego or vainglory or wealth. We simply pray for enough time to teach and guide others in their search for soul's perfection. We shall keep this great truth in mind as we deal with others: I am glad that I am me, and I am glad that You are You. Help us, Dear God, to pull others along, and maybe then they will feel the peace of Your presence walking beside them. Amen.

peace and grace

Dear God, I ask for the golden light of Christ to come around me. I ask that I live my life with the purest motive that is aligned with my own chart. And if there is any way that my chart can be modified to help me, I ask for You, Mother God, to aid and abet, as well as the archetypes, the archangels, my guides, the Council, and the throng of entities that come around when I ask.

Let me feel God's energy flowing through me, unfettered, without the ignorance, hypocrisy, or false trepidation we have been given. May I feel the peace and the glory of God, and may my soul magnify the Lord. All the insignificant things I have worried over, all the despair that I have had, I throw into a pit and give them up to the Light, saying to myself, "All will pass, everything will pass." Soon, quicker than the blink of an eye, we will be together on the Other Side having a wonderful time, so proud of ourselves to have lived our life with prudence, justice, and right thinking. Let us bring truth to the world, no matter how small, and let it grow like an inkblot of brilliant purple light that spreads over this world—not with fear, but with love, kindness, and goodness. We ask this in the name of the Mother, the Father, the Holy Spirit, and the Christ-consciousness. Amen.

prayer to
be in God's service

Dear God, we ask You for the enlightenment to be able to heal, to be able to give Your word out, to give us strength, to maintain a peace of mind that will stay in our hearts.

All-healing God, we ask to go out to all the people who need our help, all the people who are named in our hearts, and even those people who will remain nameless to us. Whether they are poor; deprived in a foreign country; homeless; or persecuted by race, creed, or religion, we ask for help and blessing for everyone.

We ask for a ray of gold light to go into every heart that needs it. More important, Lord, we ask that all of these souls accept Your Divine light, Your comfort, and Your peace, and develop the will to go forward.

We ask to finish this life and be proud of what we have done. Just like in school, we are helping our Teacher. We add our hands, our shoulders, and our lips to Your service.

We ask this in the name of the Mother, the Father, the Son, and the Holy Spirit. Amen.

prayer for

fortitude

Dearest God, I ask you to place a
golden cross right on my forehead
and extend the stem of the cross all the
way down to the middle part of my
solar plexus, which looks like the golden
sword of Azna. I ask for my soul to rise
up and meet the truth and be free. In
my heart of hearts today, I ask that all
negativity be released. Any addictions,
phobias, pains, even old fears—I ask
that they all be released. Set me free so
I may walk with the true Christ-consciousness.

Today I petition you, Mother Azna,
for my prosperity, and to be freed from
worries. Let me carry this sword in front
of me to protect me from darkness.
Free me from the cares, trials, and

tribulations of the day. I ask that sickness stay away, that my loved ones be safe, and that I have the White Light of the Holy Spirit around me and all of my family and friends. I ask for God's hand to brush the cobwebs away from my soul. I feel secure, knowing that Father God is holding me forever in His hands; and Mother God is fighting for me, loving me, standing with me, and interceding for me. All the while, I ask that my hands are within Christ's hands, walking quietly, steadfastly to the end, to the very end of the road, and then being able to stand before God with my face lifted and say, "Dear God, with pure motive I did my best."

I ask this in the name of the Mother, the Father, and the Holy Spirit. Amen.

prayer to
flow with life

O God, time is the great healer of grief, deceit, and adversity. Is it not also the enemy of beauty, and perhaps, love?

To ensure constancy in what is really beauty and love, one must commit oneself totally to the cause, the core.

This, O God, must be the true formula—giving and loving. If not, then all dreams and hopes are fleeting and illusive.

True constancy lies in You, and Your eternal time. Amen.

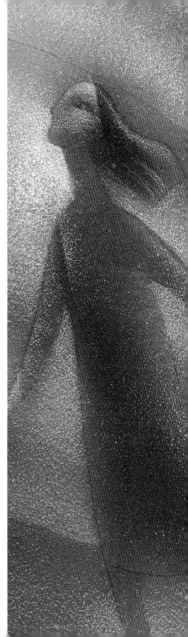

prayer for
peace of the soul

Dear God, we ask for the Holy Spirit to come down to us today, and for the Christ-consciousness to hold us close. We ask for Mother and Father God to watch over us, and for all the other archangels and archetypes to come and stand with us. We ask for the all-encompassing love of God to spread out from us, in our purity of soul, our forgiveness, and in our willingness to give and accept truth.

Let us pull in all the love and peace around us, and we ask that each and every person we love enjoy peace, health, and wealth.

Let us know that this world is only a passing, transient place—only a schoolroom, a boot camp we learn from and then leave to go Home to the Other Side. Let all of us who have lost loved ones know that we will see everyone again soon. But we ask for peace for ourselves now. We know that those on the Other Side are all right; it is for *us* that we ask for stamina, survival, peace, soul's grace, dignity, and honor, no matter what comes or assails us. As always, let us stand before God with our white plume unsullied.

We ask this in the name of the Mother and Father God, the Holy Spirit, and the Christ-consciousness. Amen.

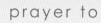

walk with the Christ-consciousness

Dear Lord, send your angels to guide us today. Help us be strong in a world that is war-torn, and filled with hypocrisy, greed, and evil. Through the desert of our lives, give us drink. Through starvation, give us bread. And in the darkest hours when we are alone, give us hope.

Let us stand tall, away from all of the tides that bind, and the ridiculous fears and hatreds of a vengeful god. May we drop all of those today, loving both God and ourselves. We ask that Your hand pass over us today. Light of the world that You are, bring about hope and peace for all the world. Let us make a difference, even if it is only slight.

We ask this in the name of the Mother, the Father, the Christ-consciousness, and the Holy Spirit. We ask this in Your name. Amen.

rejuvenation prayer

I would like my energy to be boosted and for all cloaks or shrouds to be removed. I am a child of God. I am free of any darkness. I have accepted the Christ-consciousness and the power of Azna, the Mother God, into my heart. My very being is illuminated in all areas. I am empowered with the will of Almighty God to be well, to be fruitful, and to be optimistic. I am resting in Your hands, in Your heart, O Mother and Father God. Please lead me, direct me, give me peace, and show me the way. Amen.

morning

Dearest Mother Azna, Queen of the Universe, please magnify our knowledge and faith. We love You and adore You, Queen Azna. We pay homage and gratitude to You this day. Thank You, Azna, for Your omnipotent presence.

We are thankful for Your love and protection. Dearest Mother, keep us safe. We feel Your love, and we, in return, also offer our hearts and souls to You.

Dearest Mother, protect us and our children. Dearest Mother, please also include us in Your mantle of protection because we are all Your children.

Mother, give us the courage to spread Your holy name—the courage, dear Azna, Queen of the Universe, to make this world turn white in Your name.

Thank You, Azna. Your love has bound us together. Blessed be Thy holy name. Amen.

evening

Dearest Azna, Queen of the Universe, Goddess that rules on the side of God, our Father, keep Your mantle of protection around us. Keep us forever in Your heart as You are in ours. Keep this Gnostic movement pure and safe so it may grow and spread Your name. Help us to keep the nurturing love that You have ordained. In doing so, dearest Mother, we can help the duality of the Father God and Mother Azna to bring us our God-centered Christ-consciousness.

If we are in darkness, Mother, give us light.

If we are in sickness, give us health.

If we are in fear, give us courage.

If we are alone, give us love.

Above all, Mother, give us peace and plenty of protection from our enemies. We ask this in Your blessed name. Amen.

morning

Dear Mother Azna, please attend to us this day. Let Your mantle of protection surround us. We come with honor and love. We come with gratitude for all You have done for us.

We also come with a promise and a commitment to love and serve and spread Your Holy Name. Help us live our lives in dedication to You. Guide us in our life plan, and keep us on track. Mother, You see our chart better than we do, so please use Your mantle to sweep clean the road we must travel.

Quell the hatred of our enemies. Stop the flow of greed, avarice, and deception in our lives, and make us also pure and receptive to Your love. Amen.

festival of lights prayer:

candle lighting

Dear Azna, accept this light as a symbol of the light of my soul that is reflected in this dark

64

world. Let the flame grow larger until it joins with other lights and becomes a halo of light, a refuge for all those who toil in darkness and suffering.

Today, use the light of our candles to light all the dark corners of this world.

We love You, Azna.

We adore You, Azna.

Keep us in Your arms forever. Amen.

festival of lights prayer:

evening

Dear Mother, not just for today, but for all the days and nights of our life, attend to us. Visit us often. Our doors are always open to Your blessed face. Take with You today our lights, and add them to the halo of Your light. Forgive our wrongs against ourselves. Free us from the guilt of past programming, and leave our minds and souls and bodies free to serve You.

At the end of our life, be waiting for us, dear Azna. Give us a sword of might to cut darkness and fight the adversities of this world. Give us courage to profess our faith and knowledge so we will be an example to all who come. Amen.

prayer for

house blessing and cleansing

In the name of our Heavenly Father, the Holy Mother, and the Divine Son, we ask that the Holy Spirit cleanse and purify this room so that no darkness can remain or enter. Encompass this room completely and wholly with your love and your protection. Amen.

Note: *After all the rooms are blessed, the following prayer should be said for the individuals:*

Dear God, let all who reside in and enter this home be imbued with Your love, protection, and light. Amen.

morning

Dearest Mother, today we symbolically bring our offerings that represent what our needs are for the next year, what we wish to harvest not only for our minds and bodies, but the harvesting of the spirituality of our souls as well.

As You have for centuries, dearest Mother, attend us now. Show Your power and might, and the power of Your justice.

We ask that You harvest from our souls all adversity, and that the wounds from our battles here on Earth be healed. We ask that this mantle of Your Earth yield up plenty for our needs. We ask that You give us the courage to go forth, and harvest souls toward Your light. Give us the knowledge, with our Father's help, to be eloquent, and bring souls toward the light of Your godliness.

Mother, remember our name. Mother, look down upon us. Mother, protect us. Mother, let Your gifts of bounty come to us. Let us be free from guilt, fear, and greed—and let us be able to share our heart's wealth with each other.

We ask this in Your holy name. Amen.

evening

Dearest Azna and Father God, attend to us with Your bountiful gifts for the coming year. We are in our hearts and souls as one, coming before You as Your anointed ones. Glean from the harvest of our souls—our good acts as the Gnostics of old. Weigh them before our acts of adversity, and see that our hearts are pure. Help us to avoid judging ourselves or others. Keep us pure of heart and purpose. Stay with us, Mother, as we praise and honor Your name.

We petition our Lord God and our Christ-consciousness, and let the light of the Holy Spirit shine upon us. Thank You, Mother. Blessed be Thy Holy Name. Amen.

prayer to

our beloved
Mother God, Azna

My beloved Azna, let Your mantle surround us and protect us. Our Mother, we address You as the miracle worker, the glorious vehicle of intercession and healing support.

We petition You as the Queen and Guardian of the world, to bring Your grace and beneficence into our lives.

We adore and honor You as the companion to our blessed Creator, God the Father. We accept You as the counterpart to our creation and give our hearts and souls to You in service.

We know You can help us fulfill our preordained chart for our own perfection. We also know that we may petition You for our needs and desires. [State your petition.]

Dearest Glorious Mother, Queen of the Universe, our love is endless, and our devotion is unwavering. Protect us from the failings of our own egos. Protect us from the negativities of life and the darkness that can surround us.

Let Your light of emotional understanding be a reflective shield against any evil.

If we fail to remember You each day, dearest Mother, remember us, and be waiting for us at the end of our lives so we can behold Your glorious countenance.

We ask this in the name of the Mother, Father, and Christ-consciousness. Amen.

prayer to

parents and teachers

Please encourage your children to be open to the fact that God is ever-present. Mother God is the protector, and Father God is steadfast, static, and unmovable.

Encourage them to surround themselves with the White Light, as well as walking with the Light of Christ.

In this day and age of horrible happenings, our children must not only be given our protection, but must be aware of a higher power and God's omnipotent love.

If they have this to carry as a torch, it will light their way in a dark world.

God bless and protect the children. Amen.

a child's prayer

Dear Mother and Father God, please keep me close to Your heart and protect me always.

Keep all darkness away from me. Keep the White Light of the Holy Spirit around me, which is God's love for me.

I ask that Father God hold me close, with His arms around me. I ask that my guardian angel stay with me always and protect me all of my life.

I ask that I will forever be able to hear the voice of God and my angels in my heart. Amen.

morning

Dearest Mother Azna, bless this Winter Solstice. Bless this time of quiet and introspection. Bless us with the colors of Nature that You guard. Bless this earth and those of us who still struggle here. Please surround us with Your grace.

This, dear Mother, we ask in Your Holy Name. We also call on the name of Jesus, our Christ-consciousness; our Father, who is with us; and the Divine Light of the Holy Spirit.

The colors we ask our auras to emulate are:

- green, for *healing*
- purple, for *sanctity*
- gold, for *higher consciousness*
- blue, for *tranquility*
- white, for *protection*

We want all these colors to surround us, but we ask to receive a special color today that dominates our auras—to manifest our needs throughout the year.

Bless us, Mother. We ask this in Your Holy Name. Amen.

midday

Dear Azna, we ask to receive Your light, and ask that You imbue us with grace, honor, and loyalty. We ask that You be omnipresent in our lives throughout this year and the years that follow.

We ask that we, Your daughters and sons of this earth, follow in the path of our Lord, Jesus Christ, and through Your light, experience for God, our Father. Keep us protected throughout the year. Give us the grace to face all darkness and adversity. We ask that Your Golden Sword protect us from all our enemies. Amen.

winter solstice prayer:
evening

Dear Mother Azna, please know us by name. Know our faces and know our hearts. Make us strong throughout this year so that no matter what adversity comes, we are able to handle it. Know that this life is only transient, and that it is a passing "star" in a dark night.

We also ask as we pass through this dark night of life that we be like a streaking comet, that we give off brilliance so that everyone that follows after us will be able to know us, that the name of Gnosticism will be on everyone's lips; and Your name, dearest Mother, will be heralded throughout the world.

Again, we ask this in the name of our Lord, Jesus; Father God; Mother God; in the Christ-consciousness; and the Holy Spirit. Amen.

pillar of light prayer

Dear God, we do not ask that You or Your Son, Jesus Christ, descend to us. We want to ascend to You. We want to lift our hearts and spirits together as one, traveling up this golden thread—which is our soul—like a pillar of light, so that grace travels both ways. Let us feel ourselves ascend higher and higher to Your blessing, to Your grace, surrounding us in a purple flame, rinsing out all the negativity and all the hurts and disappointments we have gone through during this year.

May we bask in the blessing of all the good that we have done, and feel the peace that descends now as we ascend higher and higher. Let this pillar of light shoot out of the room and begin to rise higher in the sky, because we want the power and thrust of this to go higher and higher like a beacon of light, showing everyone in our world that Novus Spiritus does have the answers. Let us be more and more convicted that our soul is dedicated to the thrust of this mission, to make a resolution now to rid the world of guilt and pain and devils and fear. Let our thread of golden light attach to this pillar of light. May we make the pillar wider, larger, and bigger, so that as each new thread attaches, it becomes higher and larger until it spreads everywhere. Amen.

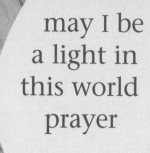

may I be a light in this world prayer

Dear Azna, surround me with Your golden light and protect me with Your sword, as You are the companion of God. Surround me with the purple light of Christ, the white light of purity, God-consciousness, and the Holy Spirit. Let me feel the expansion in my soul. And regardless of where I come from and what I believe, I make witness to Your Light, Dear Lord. I make witness to my belief and my continued search for knowledge and truth.

Dear God, let me love You enough. Let my love grow every single day and permeate every single cell of my body and soul so that when I walk through darkness, the light falls off of me, springs from me, and touches all who come near me. All the souls out there who are despairing, let me heal. All the people who are sick, let me minister to them. All the people who feel loveless, let me love. All the people who feel alienated, bring them to me. I ask to be a shepherd. I ask to be a minister to my faith and belief, and more important, my knowledge.

As I stand before You, God, I ask to feel our Lord approaching with his arms outstretched, and in front of him is a red ruby-colored rose, which he hands to me. Let me hold it close to my breast and feel the color, the light, the spirit, and the grace invade every part of me. Let it become so magnificent that it stretches out from my arms and my hands in a healing glory.

I ask this, dear God, in the name of the Mother, the Father, the Son, and the Holy Spirit. Amen.

wedding prayer

Love is God's complete triangle, welding both souls to the glory of Them.

Love is, and should be, the outward manifestation of God's goodness, shining through the union of two people.

Love cannot grow in quiet darkness, nor survive in too much brilliant light. It cannot survive in silence or in screams.

Love must be tempered and nurtured; it can even be watered with some tears, as well as bloom with laughter. Stagnation kills love—leaving it devoid of attention.

Grow in Love [insert names] _____ and _____, and in this love, you will shine for each other and become a beacon of light for others.

Love is forever giving, forever comforting, never self-centered in motive. It is truly a complete triangle, with God at its apex.

_____ and _____, we here are aware of your love and know that no matter what desert or valley you encounter, you will see it through together.

Let the Love that shines for you both today blend with ours to keep it bright. For as long as love exists, then the essence of God exists within us.

God bless you both.

prayer for
funerals or
graduations
(going from one life to the next)

Dear Mother and Father God, we ask for this soul to transcend. We ask for this soul to be bathed in Your Holy Light. We ask for the tunnel to open wide, and for our loving Mother Azna to embrace the person who is graduating from this life to be embraced to find their peace, their loved ones, and all people who have been in other lives.

We ask for blessings to be upon all of those gathered who are left behind, but we know, with the grace of God and with all assuredness, that we will all be together soon. We ask for peace to descend on all whom are left grieving today so they can be embraced by the mantle of our Holy Mother, Azna. May the Christ-consciousness attend them in their grief, and may the Holy Spirit surround them. Amen.

prayer to
stave off loneliness

Dearest God, You are my anchor and my salvation in this time of trial. I will receive the Holy Light of Mother Azna and the steadfastness of Your constancy. I expect and demand to feel Your love fill up my heart, mind, and soul to rid my mind from any feelings of loneliness, rejection, and despondency. In asking for Your Holy Light to fill up my soul, mind, and heart, there can be no room for darkness. Amen.

(Repeat twice.)

prayer to

release addictions

(For any addiction: overeating, drinking, smoking,
nail-biting—and even addiction to a person)

Dear Mother and Father God, please help me unlatch my soul from any physical needs so that I may be free from all the things that hold me to worldly pleasures and that may harm me. Please release them from my soul and mind as if they never existed. Please also heal any harm that I may have done from any physical addictions. I petition You, Azna, to use Your Golden Sword to cut through the need and the want of any substance that I cannot seem to release myself from.

I ask this in the name of the Father, Mother, Son, and Holy Spirit. Amen.

prayer to
eliminate despair

Dearest Mother and Father God, my despair feels like a tangible force, so engulfing that it encompasses my thoughts. Knowing this and in the acceptance of it, allow me to ride it through and come out on the other side, brighter and unscathed.

I realize that reaching the depths of my soul's sorrow is a ferocious lesson, but I will, with Your mighty sword, triumph over my pain, loss, and suffering. I will see Your Golden Sword cut through the cobwebs of my mind and bring light to my desert. Amen.

a comforting prayer

May God, our Mother and Father, and the Christ-consciousness always be with us. On this journey, let us keep the White Light of the Holy Spirit around us always, and even though we have written our chart, may we know that there are miracles. Amen.

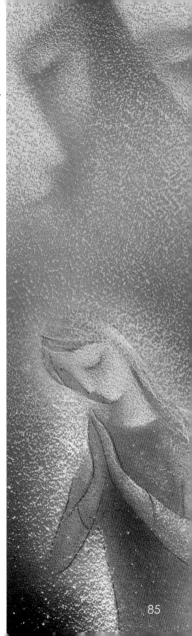

Novus Spiritus
celebrations

(Equinox, Solstice, and Special festivals)

*(To be celebrated on the
Sunday nearest to the date)*

Spring Equinox Solstice—March 21

The time of new beginnings.

Blessing of the Children—May 30

Annual Gnostic blessing
for the children.

Summer Solstice—June 21

The time in which all the faithful
bring gifts and coins in honor
of benefits received.

Festival of Lights—August 21

A time of celebration for the early
Gnostics who wanted to pay homage
to the Mother Goddess (Who was also
the symbol of fertility for humans,
for the earth, and for all growing things).
Candles are a symbol of the soul.

Autumn Equinox—September 21

Not only the time of harvest, but also
the time of giving honor and homage
to the earth, which is the domain
and dominion of the Mother Goddess.

Mother Azna's Feast Day—December 8

Our testimonial to our Blessed Mother.
(Submit petitions and special
prayers to Azna.)

Winter Solstice—December 21

This is the time of remembrance, a time
of quiet and introspection for the year that has
passed and the lessons we have learned.
This is the time to bury all of the old pain,
guilt, illness, and fear under a white mantle
of snow, which will purify deeds we have
done, or deeds done to us. In this way, it is
a time of remembrance and a time
of forgetting and forgiving.

About the Author

Millions of people have witnessed **Sylvia Browne's** incredible psychic powers on TV shows such as *Montel, Larry King Live, Entertainment Tonight,* and *Unsolved Mysteries;* and she has been profiled in *Cosmopolitan, People* magazine, and other national media. Her on-target psychic readings have helped police solve crimes, and she astounds audiences wherever she appears.

She is also the founder of the **Society of Novus Spiritus,** a community of Gnostic Christians that provides:

- counseling
- hypnosis
- regressions
- classes
- church services
- study group programs . . . and more!

For further information about Sylvia or Novus Spiritus, please contact **www.sylvia.org** or:

Sylvia Browne Corp., 35 Dillon Ave., Campbell, CA 95008 • (408) 379-7070

Also by
Sylvia Browne

Books/Card Deck

Adventures of a Psychic
(with Antoinette May)

Astrology Through a Psychic's Eyes

*Blessings from the Other Side**

Conversations with the Other Side

Heart and Soul (card deck)

A Journal of Love and Healing
(with Nancy Dufresne)

*Life on the Other Side**

Meditations

The Other Side and Back
(with Lindsay Harrison)*

Past Lives, Future Healing

and . . .

My Life with Sylvia Browne
(by Sylvia's son, Chris Dufresne)

The **Journey of the Soul** *Series*
(available individually or in a boxed set)
God, Creation, and Tools for Life (Book 1)
Soul's Perfection (Book 2)
The Nature of Good and Evil (Book 3)

Audios

Angels and Spirit Guides
Healing Your Body, Mind, and Soul
Life on the Other Side (audio book)*
Making Contact with the Other Side
The Other Side of Life
Sylvia Browne's Tools for Life

(All of the above titles are
available at your local bookstore.
Those without asterisks may also be
ordered by calling Hay House at
760-431-7695 or 800-654-5126.)

About the Artist

Christina Simonds is on the staff at Sylvia Browne's office and is an ordained minister of the Society of Novus Spiritus, the church founded by Sylvia Browne. She is also an illustrator who sees her work as a means to convey the Gnostic Christian philosophy through symbolism within her art. She lives in the Santa Cruz mountains of Northern California, and works with her brother Kirk Simonds, also an illustrator—both of whom have published artwork in Sylvia Browne's book *Life on the Other Side* (Dutton, 2000).

Christina is available for personalized drawings. If you would like her to make an angel out of your favorite person, or to purchase reprints of the drawings in this book, please visit her Website at: **www.christinasimonds.com.**

About the Artist

Since his emigration from Russia to the U.S. in 1990, recognition of **Leonid Gore's** enormous talent has spread throughout the publishing world. Critics have praised his work as visually stunning, astonishing, brilliant, haunting, misty, moody, and dreamlike. His paintings have regularly been shown at the prestigious and competitive annual exhibitions of the Society of Illustrators in New York. Mr. Gore; his wife, Nina; and their young daughter, Emily; live in Brooklyn.

Please visit **hkportfolio.com** for more information about Leonid Gore's work.

Other Hay House Lifestyles Titles of Related Interest

Books

A Garden of Thoughts,
by Louise L. Hay

Dream Journal,
by Leon Nacson

Inner Wisdom,
by Louise L. Hay

Interpreting Dreams A–Z,
by Leon Nacson

The Love and Power Journal,
by Lynn V. Andrews

Pleasant Dreams,
by Amy E. Dean

Simple Things,
by Jim Brickman

What Is Spirit?,
by Lexie Brockway Potamkin

You Can Heal Your Life Gift Edition,
by Louise L. Hay

Card Decks

The Four Agreements Cards,
by DON Miguel Ruiz

Healing with the Angels Oracle Cards
(booklet and card deck),
by Doreen Virtue, Ph.D.

Healing with the Fairies Oracle Cards
(booklet and card deck),
by Doreen Virtue, Ph.D.

Inner Peace Cards,
by Dr. Wayne W. Dyer

MarsVenus Cards,
by John Gray

Miracle Cards,
by Marianne Williamson
(available January 2002)

Power Thought Cards,
by Louise L. Hay

Power Thoughts for Teens,
by Louise L. Hay

Wisdom Cards,
by Louise L. Hay

Zen Cards,
by Daniel Levin

All of the above titles may be ordered by calling
Hay House at the numbers on the next page.

We hope you enjoyed
this Hay House Lifestyles book.
If you would like to receive a
free catalog featuring additional
Hay House books and products, or if
you would like information about the
Hay Foundation, please contact:

Hay House, Inc.
P.O. Box 5100
Carlsbad, CA 92018-5100

(760) 431-7695 or **(800) 654-5126**
(760) 431-6948 (fax) or **(800) 650-5115 (fax)**
www.hayhouse.com

Hay House Australia Pty Ltd
P.O. Box 515
Brighton-Le-Sands, NSW 2216
phone: 1800 023 516
e-mail: info@hayhouse.com.au